# Hydroponic Gardening

## A Beginner Guide to Learn How to Design and Build Your Own Sustainable Hydroponics System, for Growing Plants and Vegetables at Home

**Terri Carr**

free of responsibility as to the actions taken outside of their direct purview. Regardless, there are zero scenarios where the original author or the Publisher can be deemed liable in any fashion for any damages or hardships that may result from any of the information discussed herein.

Additionally, the information in the following pages is intended only for informational purposes and should thus be thought of as universal. As befitting its nature, it is presented without assurance regarding its prolonged validity or interim quality. Trademarks that are mentioned are done without written consent and can in no way be considered an endorsement from the trademark holder.

# CHAPTER ONE
## How plants work in Hydroponics

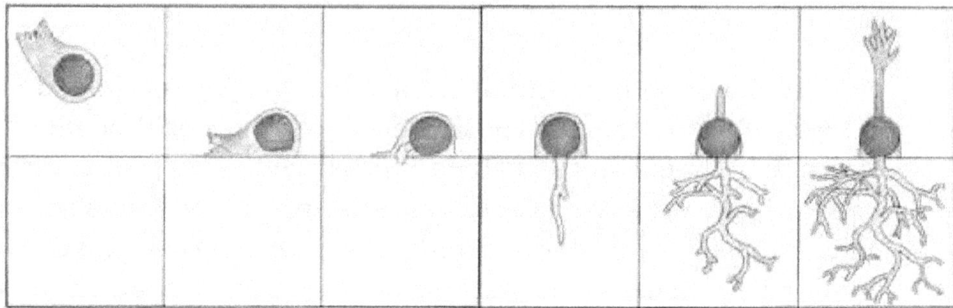

Probably the most important prerequisite for running any Hydroponic system successfully is a clear understanding of how the plants work. With this knowledge, you will be able to see why the component parts of a hydroponic system are included, and why certain actions will produce better growth in the plants, while others may be detrimental to their health.

How Plants Grow

A young root tip evolves from a seed that pushes down its direction into the soil.

You will quickly gain an understanding of how most plants work by looking at how trees grow. The story begins with the seed that is the dispersal unit within a tree's life cycle. Each autumn, the parent trees scatter thousands of seeds across the forest floor, sprouting later in spring.

Germination starts when the dry seed draws off the soil in water and the seed softens and swells. A few days later, by cell division, a tiny root will grow, developing into a visible root that emerges through the seed coat, bends downwards and enters the soil. Then the root grows tiny root hairs, by which the new tree absorbs the water it requires for growth. The minerals which the developing tree requires are dissolved in the water. In a few weeks, branch roots start to develop, which would in turn will chuck off more branch roots as they evolve stouter.

Surprisingly the root system remains shallow. Deep tap roots are rare, for roots in the surface layers of the soil fulfill their functions best. The growth in the size and substance of the roots of a tree is maintained through the healthy function of the green leaves of the tree.

## Photosynthesis

A few days after the seed emerged from the first roots and made their way underground the seed would also have produced its first small shoot. All seeds of the tree contain one or more leaves of seed, called cotyledons. The upward growth of the first little shoot of the tree continues for the remainder of its life. The aerial shoots like the tree's roots are nourished on the shoots by the leaves which develop. Photosynthesis is named the key process. This literally means' making up with the help of light' translated from its Greek language. Photosynthesis is essentially the process through which plants trap and utilize light energy.

Green plants appear green, reflecting green light and absorbing the other colors which make up' white' light. Chlorophyll is the pigment that gives plants this green colour, and this substance is mainly used to trap light.

Chlorophyll that regulates the photosynthetic reaction is found in different cells in the leaves called chloroplasts. Plants need to absorb sunlight, because it gives them the energy they need to produce the food they need for growth.

## The Production of Food in a Plant's Leaves

The leaves on a plant are constantly filtering a stream of air through their tissues, which are open-textured with many air passages. Air consists of about four parts of nitrogen to one of oxygen, plus a tiny but significant amount of carbon dioxide. The plant needs carbon to create new tissues producing what we see as growth. The chlorophyll in the leaves, using energy from sunlight, extracts the carbon dioxide from the air and combines it with water to make chemicals called carbohydrates.

A familiar type of carbohydrate is sugar. Glucose sugar is a soluble type of carbohydrate produced by photosynthesis that is able to flow freely throughout the plant providing the food necessary to nourish every kind of growth and also supply the energy for every vital process. The leaves, shoots, roots, the woody stem, flowers and finally the fruit and seeds are all built up from it. Plants use the energy stored in carbohydrates through a process called respiration.

You can see that photosynthesis is an important process for plants for without it the carbohydrates or sugars needed by the plant for growth, would not be produced. It is also an important process for humans because during the process of trapping light energy, oxygen is separated from water and released into the atmosphere. Green plants therefore remove the carbon dioxide that humans and other animals breathe into the air and release the oxygen we depend on to survive.

## Transpiration

Between 80 and 95 percent of a plant's weight is made up of water. Plants take in supplies of water through their roots losing up to 98 percent of their water intake through a process called transpiration. This occurs when the air passing through the passages in the plant's leaves carries away large quantities of water. The flow of air is necessary so that the plant can obtain the carbon needed to produce carbohydrates. The plant also needs to maintain its water supply. It is not surprising therefore that the root systems of plants are extremely efficient at extracting water from the soil while other structures within the plant can efficiently transport it against the force of gravity, up to 100 metres high in some trees.

There are two main types of vessels that allow water and nutrients to flow upward from the roots in the form of sap, and carbohydrate solution to flow through the whole plant. The xylem vessels contain the sap that flows up into the leaves from the roots, while the phloem vessels contain the carbohydrates produced in the leaves that flow around the plant and down to the roots where they can be converted to starches and stored. In most plants these two-way pathways, the xylem and phloem are organized into vascular bundles that run up within the stem of the plant. Upon reaching the leaves of the plant they take the form of veins.

The xylem and phloem are arranged in branches and trunks of trees, in a different pattern. They are grouped underneath the bark on either side of a layer of cells, called the cambio. The root sap rises on the inside of the cambium layer while on the outer side of the cambium layer the carbohydrates or sugar sap descends through the Phloem tissues called Bast.

On this side of the cambium layer, the carbohydrate solution produces new growth which, when combined with a shrinking of these cells in the summer, forms the growth rings visible when you cut through a tree. The cells open again each spring allowing the sap to escape, and a new ring of change growth to emerge under the bark.

The xylem in plants carries not only water but also dissolved minerals into the water. For healthy growth, plants need the most, if not all, of at least seventeen different elements. Nine of these elements; large amounts of carbon, hydrogen, oxygen, nitrogen, phosphorus, potassium, sulphur, calcium, and magnesium are required, called macro nutrients.

The first three: carbon, hydrogen and oxygen from carbon dioxide and water, the rest from soil.

The remaining seven nutrients known as micro nutrients or trace elements are required in smaller quantities but are still crucial to healthy growth of the plants. These are titanium, manganese, boron, zinc, molybdenum, copper, and chlorine. If the plant is unavailable for any of these mineral nutrients then the growth of the plant will suffer in some way.

Some soils are lacking in some aspects, so that plants grown in them show the symptoms of deficiency of the elements they lack. Even in the soil the product may be present but not in a soluble form that will allow the plant to absorb it. That is one of the reasons why plants grown hydroponically produce fast, healthy growth. All the nutrients they require are always available in the right proportions, as is the all-important supply of water to which the nutrients are dissolved.

The process by which plants absorb the mineral nutrients dissolved in water is called osmosis. The tendency of fluids to pass through a semi-permeable membrane and mix with each other is osmosis. A semi-permeable membrane is something that enables it to move through some things but not others. In plants, the small hairs on the roots require nutrients dissolved in water to reach the root system but, for example, do not permit particles of soil to enter the plant.

Osmosis is a major mechanism found in plants and animals alike. Digested food is osmosised into the bloodstream in animals. The cells in a plant's root hairs contain a dense solution of salts and organic acids. Because this solution is stronger than the weak solution of nutrients dissolved in water in the soil, there is a robust osmotic pressure driving the weak solution in through the cell walls to mix with the dense solution. This process of osmosis continues from cell to cell so that the nutrients dissolved in water in the soil enter the plant's roots, eventually moving through the whole plant.

Osmosis can also work in reverse and kill a plant. Some gardeners when they apply a heavy dosing of soluble fertiliser around a plant create a situation where the solution in the soil is stronger than in the plant. As a result the plant loses its moisture, wilts and often dies. Because the nutrient solution being fed to hydroponically grown plants can be metered, this situation is easily avoided.

Plants grown hydroponically, receiving the nutrients they require, may even develop to a degree not normally reached by plants grown in the soil. Their roots become extremely well nourished, accumulating large quantities of mineral salts. Because the solution of salts in the plants root cells is so strong the ability of these cells to take up water is increased. So instead of water and nutrients moving up through the plants xylem by osmosis, so much water may be taken in by the roots that the water is forced up the Xylem. The roots actually act as a pump. This condition has been termed 'root pressure' and accelerates the development of the rest of the plant.

## Growth Hormones

Further research into the way plants grow has made it possible for the rate of plant growth to be even further accelerated. Generally growth in a plant occurs at different rates in different parts of the plant. Some parts of the plant will grow at similar rates, the roots and shoots do not outgrow each other because they are interdependent. They both need each other, the shoots need minerals obtained by the roots and the roots need the photosynthetic products of the leaves on the shoots. There are special messenger molecules in plants known as hormones which control the rates of growth in plants.

Hormones are generated in various parts of a plant and are transported in minute amounts around the plant affecting the type of growth taking place in the cells that plants are made up of. Synthetic hormones are now available which can be included in a hydroponic growers nutrient solution to produce the increased growth attributable to some of these hormones. Flowering and fruiting are two critical developments in a plant's growth in which hormones are involved. Hormones respond to changes in the environment stimulating flowering and fruiting. Flowering for example is often controlled by the day length, a response known as photoperiodism. Flower growers can now induce flowering at almost any time of the year with equipment regulating the amount of light to their plants, and growth hormones.

# CHAPTER TWO

## The Essential Nutrients

### Nitrogen

Nitrogen is one of the principal elements that contribute to a plant's growth. Plants use nitrogen to create amino acids and proteins that are used to generate new growth in cells. Nitrogen quickly travels throughout the plant to promote new growth at the detriment of the older foliage. Any deficiency will cause weakness in the new growth and spindly result in a stunted plant. The shortage is usually first noticeable in older leaves of a plant which lose their green color and gradually turn yellow. This is because nitrogen is essential in the leaves for the green oxygen which produces chlorophyll pigment.

The small leaves will also be yellow as the scarcity persists and the veins on the underside of the leaves turn a red or purple colour. Vegetable plants may run to seed. An abundance of nitrogen will also affect the fruiting or seed production of most plants

## Phosphorus

Another essential plant growth factor, phosphorus, is also crucial for plant photosynthesis and cell forming. It acts as a catalyst facilitating energy transfer for the plant, in this case. Phosphorus is important in the development of good root systems, and is also needed to form the flowers and seeds of a plant. Because phosphorus, like nitrogen, is very mobile within the plant, any deficiency is usually visible in the color of the plant's leaves. Deficiency of phosphorus produces a deep green colouring of the leaf.

## Potassium

Potassium, like phosphorus, acts as a catalyst for activating or triggering a number of plant functions within plants. It is a source for plant enzymes that ward off disease and play an important role in the development of cells.

The mottling of older leaves on plants and yellowing of leaves along their veins may suggest a deficiency in potassium. It is another item in the plant that is mobile so the older leaves first display any deficiencies. Plants which lack this nutrient may lose their fruit before it matures.

## Calcium

Calcium is the element that supports cell walls as they form in plants. It helps buffer other elements ' excesses, and is an important part of the root structure of a plant. Calcium in plants is not very mobile so it is present in older growth in greater concentration. As a result, when there is a calcium deficiency it is the new growth which first suffers. The older growth preserves its calcium but this important element will be short of new growth. The fresh tips of the leaves and the rising points tend to die back with a calcium deficiency and the leaves have a brown to black scorching, even low calcium is the source of blossom end rot, often seen as a black scab on the tomato fruit bottom.

## Magnesium

Another factor essential for photosynthesis in plants is magnesium. It is vitally important for the chlorophyll molecule and is also widely used in seed production. A deficiency can yellow in the leaves of a plant and spread from the center to the outer edges of the leaf. The leaves eventually turn an orange colour. A lack of magnesium gives rise to further issues if you want to grow additional plants from the seeds being produced as they are malformed and have a poor germination rate. Magnesium acts as a phosphorus carrier within the plant and encourages the formation of oils, fats, and juice.

## Sulfur

As with calcium, sulphur is important in the tissue structure of a plant. It is one of the plant protein components and plays an important part in producing most plants ' flavors and odors. When the younger leaves on a plant become pale, a lack of sulphur appears. Despite continuing growth, it tends to be hard and woody with very little increase in radial growth. Within a plant, sulfur does not move around much.

## Iron

Iron is required for chlorophyll production in plants and is used in photosynthesis. An iron deficiency will affect new growth of the plants, the leaves will become almost white and the leaf veins will show a definite yellowing.

Iron is not very mobile or easily absorbed within plants making it a problem element to replace once lost. Iron is an important micronutrient that all plants and animals need.

## Manganese

Manganese is involved in many plant enzymes, particularly those which reduce nitrates before protein production. The mottled yellowing of younger leaves will generally characterize a shortage of manganese. Especially on citrus trees, only small, yellow leaves form and develop no further. It's also affected the formation of new bloom buds.

## Zinc

Zinc is a part of growth hormones and is essential for most plant enzymes, too. Zinc is another element that once lost isn't easily replaced. The new, zinc-deficient plant leaves are highly undersized. Zinc increases the energy source for chlorophyll production, and also promotes water absorption. This is partly why plants which lack zinc may be stunted. Also partly dependent on the presence of zinc is the formation of auxins, hormones which promote growth in plant cells.

## Copper

Plants use copper as an activator or catalyst for various important enzymes. A lack of copper will cause new growth to wane, or sometimes irregular growth, often with new shoots dying back. Sometimes, fruit can break during maturity, particularly at warm temperatures. Copper increases the sugar content of citrus fruit and makes crops such as carrots, spinach and apples more colorful. When haemoglobin is formed in animal blood, copper is important in the use of iron.

## Boron

In this element, boron deficiency is generally shown by the slow death of plant tissue especially around the main growing point and the roots ' apex or center point. On the fruit of plants lacking in boron appear cracks varying from small to fairly large in size. Quite often the roots become hollow and deteriorate. As well as being important for pollination and seed production, boron is necessary for normal cell division and protein formation.

## Molybdenum

Molybdenum is used by plants in the formation of proteins and affects the ability of the plant to fix atmospheric nitrogen. Pale leaves which appear burnt towards the edges may suggest a deficiency. Sometimes, the leaves may get distorted. Broccoli, Brussels sprouts, lettuce, cauliflower, and other brassicas will not adequately grow leaves when molybdenum is unavailable. Molybdenum is also essential for plants such as peas that use nitrogen fixing bacteria to have nodules on their roots. Only after detailing the functions of these nutrient elements can it be concluded that they are all vital to the production of healthy plants.

You may wonder how plants may thrive in the soil where in varying degrees one or more of those essential elements may be deficient. Plants grow extremely well in the wild, uncontaminated by humans. Only plants which are suitable for extremely poor soils will grow on those soils. In addition, plants gradually modify the soil by breaking it up with their root systems, some even help to replace nutrients in the soil, for example, peas have nitrogen-fixing bacteria in the legumes at their roots. Some plant species are bound to become established even in the most deficient soils, paving the way for other species which may succeed them later on.

Complex plant communities develop frequently, such as the New Zealand native forests, feeding large amounts of humus into the soil as old growth breaks down to make way for new growth. The native trees ' intricate root systems retain this fertile soil in place while the thick cover offered by their leaves keeps it moist and humid, creating the ideal conditions for ferns and other undergrowths.

If left alone, plants respond to their surroundings and change it very effectively, the difficulties arise when people try to support large numbers of people, set up complex monocultures. Single crop varieties are cultivated over large areas, allowing large-scale application of pesticides to remove rivals and other chemicals for disease control. The remaining humus in the soil from bygone native forests will soon be spent requiring ongoing large-scale fertilizer applications that may provide plants with the nutrients they need but do not replace the function of humus in keeping the soil in a light, aerated, workable condition.

During the construction process, the home gardener is put in a similar position on a new section that had all but the minimum amount of topsoil required to grow a layer of grass. Topsoil (and compost) must be returned to form a vegetable garden or fruit trees. It takes fertilizers and compost to bring up the humic content in the soil. However, the home gardener is hampered by the lack of technical guidance from the experts who are often employed to examine the soil conditions where substantial cropping is performed and recommend the appropriate fertilizer applications. Prevention is better than cure for the home gardener wanting to grow a variety of crops, the solution being to keep feeding a steady supply of fertilizer and compost into the vegetable garden soil rather than waiting for the signs of deficiency described earlier to emerge.

Hydroponic production reduces the issues associated with poor soil and is low in nutrients for commercial and domestic crops alike. Instead of spending large quantities of fertilizers on a large area of soil where crops are to be grown, the commercial grower can cycle the required quantities within a compact hydroponic system by adding more nutrients only as needed.

Hydroponic systems reduce the problems faced by home gardeners when a fertilizer added to one plant community counteracts another fertilizer applied to multiple nearby plants. It is also easy to nourish plants in large quantities. Some important factors need to be present in small amounts because too high a concentration can be toxic to plants. Excellent hydroponic nutritional products made for the crop being grown contain the right nutrients in the right proportions for optimal growth, and can be easily measured and measured with inexpensive, efficient and readily available equipment.

# CHAPTER THREE
## The nutrient formula

Now that you have an appreciation of the role the different nutrient elements play in plants, and an idea of the poor plant health brought about by deficiencies of these vital elements, I can describe a typical nutrient formula to you, so that you can get some insight into the way these elements are made available to your plants in a hydroponic growing system. The essential elements comprising the nutrient mixtures are Nitrogen, Calcium, Potassium, Phosphorus, Boron, Copper, Iron, Manganese, Magnesium, Zinc, Sulphur and Molybdenum.

There are a number of other elements known to science which also play a part in the growth of plants. Among these are Sodium, Selenium, Chlorine, Vanadium and Cobalt. These elements are generally not included in the nutrient mix, since they are required in extremely small amounts, so small in fact that sufficient quantities are almost certainly present in the mixture by way of impurities. There may well be other elements which are also required, again in microscopic amounts, however, the presence of these elements as impurities is so small as to be extremely difficult to detect. Some elements are also derived from sources other than the nutrient mix. The air supplies some of these, as also does the water supply.

There are two approaches to obtaining your nutrient mixture, you can buy it in ready mixed powder form from a number of suppliers or you can mix your own. If you are a commercial grower with a massive operation you will probably want to at least mix your own significant components. Some home growers who enjoy experimenting may also want to make up their own, however you will find it easier just to buy a ready made product. Unless you are using more than 100 kilograms of dry salts per year the cost savings of mixing your own will be minimal. It's like owning a car, you may enjoy driving it but there is little point in trying to save a few cents by mixing your own petrol. Anyway, here are some formulas for those who wish to use them or would like to know what the different mixtures are made up of. You will notice that the mixtures come in two parts. This is for storage purposes to prevent precipitation between the different elements making up the mixture.

**Formula Number One for 'To Waste' systems**

**Grams per 100 litre**

Bag A- Calcium Nitrate________80.9

- Bag B-Potassium Sulphate______55.4
- Potassium Phosphate__________17.7
- Ammonium Phosphate__________9.9
- Magnesium Sulphate__________46.2
- Iron EDTA__________________3.27
- Manganese Sulphate__________0.02
- Boric Acid__________________0.172
- Zinc Sulphate______________0.044
- Ammonium Molybdate________0.005

You use this formula by volume and should dissolve the elements in the quantities shown into 100 litres of water. Note: Do not attempt to dissolve the above quantities in a smaller volume of water since chemical precipitation will take place essentially destroying the nutrient)


## Formula Number Two

The following ingredient to be dissolved into two separate containers of 25 litres of clean water to make two 'stock solution' concentrates for use in recirculating systems (can also be used in 'To Waste' systems if desired)

- Bag A Calcium Nitrate____________2.5 Kg

- The following ingredients to be dissolved into 25 litres of clean water

- 

- Bag b-Potassium Nitrate____________1.5 Kg

- Mono Potassium Phosphate________0.5 Kg

- Magnesium Sulphate____________1.3 Kg

- T.E. (Trace Element) MIX______0.1 Kg (100 grams)

To make the TE (Trace Element Mix) it helps to work in greater amounts to prevent problems weighing small parts such that it makes approximately

- 10Kgs of TE mix:
- Iron Chelate
- 7.5 Kgs Manganese
- Sulphate   1.4Kgs
- Boric Acid
- Copper Sulphate
- Zinc Sulphate (Mono)
- 85 grams Ammonium
- Molybdate   20 grams

This mix now allows you to mix your own nutrients with one of them.

In addition to simplifying the mixing of the nutrient solution, the use of a complex chemical compound known as chelate, as the iron shown above, also has other benefits

A trace element when held tightly with a molecule in the form of a chelate which prevents it from reacting with other substances. Yet the nutrient is still fully available for use when the chelate is taken up by the plant. This avoids the situation that sometimes happens when using sulphates where the sulphate becomes insoluble and unusable to the crop. Similarly, a reaction with soluble phosphates may occur which will result in both the trace elements and phosphates being' locked up.' Iron in particular should be introduced into the chelate-shaped nutrient mixture. Though it is more expensive than iron salts it requires only small amounts.

Using iron salts like ferrous sulphate in your combination causes problems with iron precipitation in the system that require regular water flushing and regular nutrient solution replacement. Most of the trace elements can be introduced in chelate form into the nutrient solution with the exception of inorganic boron and molybdenum, so that they can not be chelated.

So these are the key formulations I would prescribe for nutrient mixtures. They will provide a balanced diet for fast, and above all healthy growth for your hydroponically grown plants. Now that you've got the formulations you can try to blend the one you think would suit your needs or buy a mixed ready version. When you buy your blend, all you need to do is weigh part A and part B so that you get the right ratio as defined on the package, and then apply it to the required water content.

So long as it is a reliable "two-part" combination of nutrients, outcomes will be achieved on demand. Beware of single-mix plant foods, with advertisements stating suitability for hydroponic production. There is a lot on the market that is worthless for hydroponic use, despite claims to the contrary.

# CHAPTER FOUR
## Equipment

When choosing equipment for hydroponic systems there are two important things to keep in mind. The first is that any material that contains the solution to the nutrient must be light-proof. The other thing to note is that the products that come into contact with the nutrient solution must not emit any contaminants that disturb the nutrient solution's balance.(such as the brass arm shown on the float valve) Price would certainly be essential, but these first two factors must not be overridden.

## Storage Tanks

Plastic buckets with cut off tops and plastic rubbish bins are two types of cheap and readily available holding tanks that should satisfy all the necessary specifications. Stainless steel is a suitable material, because the mineral solution does not damage it. Concrete containers may also be used but should be aged to ensure that limes and other contaminants are leached from the concrete surfaces. A sealer coat is one way to overcome that issue.

## Nutrient Lines

Food grade, PVC pipes are the most suitable material for conveying the nutrient solution. There are a variety of plastic materials which can be adapted for use as nutrient lines, just remember to make sure that they are light-proof. Black or dark coloured pipes work well in keeping out light and also assist in picking up solar heat.

## Pumps

The vibrator type, aquarium pumps work well in the venturi type, aggregate-filled systems. They can also be used in the larger systems to pressurise a tube which can then be used to feed acid into the system. This is fully described in the chapter on setting up a system. Submersible pumps are suitable but you will have to check that they do not have any metallic components which could contaminate the nutrient mixture. These pumps are available in low voltage types from around 20 watts up to types producing several horsepowers running off the mains. The average home system could be run successfully on a 40 to 60 watt pump. There are a number of pumps available for larger systems.

## Valves

Shutoff valves placed at strategic points can be handy especially in larger hydroponic systems. They will allow you to work on sections of the system without having to shut everything down. Again these valves should be made of PVC or stainless steel. Another aspect of larger systems that you will find described in the chapter on setting up is the need for a float valve or ballcock to control the replenishment of water.

It is surprising how much water plants use, so with this in mind virtually any system larger than a window box or patio type garden will need to have a water supply flowing into the nutrient solution to replace the water used. This is easily controlled by a float valve or ballcock which will stop the flow when it reaches a selected level. If the valve does not come into contact with the nutrient solution it could be made of brass or some other alloy, however I think you will find that plastic valves are generally cheaper and work better.

## Growing Containers

There is an almost limitless range of containers that you can use in a hydroponic system. If the container is not light-proof or if it is likely to contaminate the nutrient solution you can line it with plastic film. Black polythene is the cheapest and has a long useable life. Plastic drums with their tops cut off are an economical way to set up a large growing area. The drums can be placed in a row and filled with aggregate. The nutrient mixture is pumped from the holding tank through feeder pipes to each drum.

The main feeder pipe runs down the middle of the line of drums with smaller tubes branching off to each drum. When operating the nutrient will flow in near the top of the aggregate and drain down to the base of each drum. From there, the nutrient solution is channelled through drain pipes back to the holding tank. A 15mm (1/2") polythene pipe should be large enough to drain the nutrient solution from each drum back to the main drainage pipe running to the holding tank. This is a straightforward yet effective way to build up a large system with inexpensive growing containers.

For scrap value you can purchase all manner of disused containers and adapt them for use in a hydroponic system. For starters, old concrete wash-tubs are suitable for use in filled aggregate systems.

In NFT hydroponic systems, there is also a broad range of pipes and other materials which can be used as gullies. Storm water products are ideal, they can be effectively used with plastic spouting, plastic downpipes and even long run roofing products. You can drill plastic holes to allow the plants to grow by.

Use white polythene or panda film (co-extruded black and white plastic film) to conceal the gullies and leave light off the nutrient solution whilst using guttering and other materials which provide an open gully. Holes for the plants are easily made in polythene. You can even make your own wooden gullies and use polythene to line them up. Polythene can also be used by folding it up by itself and clipping the edges together with clothes pegs at the top. When either side of a plant is clipped the pegs will also help support the plant.

## C F (Conductivity) Testing Equipment

The value of the equipment analyzing the nutrient solution should now be very clear. Before the invention of testing equipment, farmers had to apply a certain amount of nutrients to a fixed volume of water which would then produce the desired strength of a nutrient solution. This could then be used for a given period before dumping and replacing it with a new, fresh mixture.

This is a wasteful practice, as it assumes all the nutrients in the solution were used by the plants during the time it was used. In fact, probably only a proportion of the nutrient elements could have been used and apart from any symptoms of deficiency shown by the plants, the grower would have had no idea when the different constituents of nutrients had run out. Now there are licensed labs where farmers can test their mixtures of nutrients.

They may use an atomic absorption spectrometer capable of analyzing the mixture of nutrients and providing a read-out of the various elements in the mixture in parts per million. This kind of technology is far too complex, costly and overly precise for the hydroponic farmers to use daily. The CF meter already described is more appropriate which measures the strength of the nutrient solution. They are easy to use and readily available to business growers and home enthusiasts alike.

There are various types of CF meters. Older, manual CF meters consist typically of two dials and a zeroing or nulling meter. The operator first measures the temperature of the solution to test the nutrient solution and then sets this on the temperature dial which usually has settings between 15 ° C and 40 ° C. Some of the nutrient solutions then fill the sample cup in the meter with. The second knob is turned until the needle in the meter drops to zero.

The CF value is indicated by that second dial's position. The meter includes a temperature adjustment, as this has a significant effect on CF reading. The CF values are generally given at a normal temperature of 20 ° C. The temperature of the nutrient solution changes for each degree Celsius, the CF value will change by around two per cent. This can make a significant difference so that the meters have to be able to make allowance for variations in temperature. New meters with automatic conductivity (CF), automatically account for temperature differences from the normal temperature measurement of 20 ° C. Such meters minimize to a minimal the checks.

There are no tests, all you have to do is plunge the meter's probe portion into the nutrient solution. The meter then registers for you the CF value, adjusted to a digital display for temperature. The only thing that the operator needs to remember is to leave it in the solution long enough for the temperature detector to evaluate the temperature correctly. Such meters are available in both line and hand held versions.

The in line units have fittings on either end to fit them into the nutrient feed pipe which supplies the growing area. The meter will then give constant CF readings on the state of the mixture of nutrients. An additional advantage provided by some suppliers is the ability to read the values in other conductivity measures such as the' EC' scale and the TDS scale (Total dissolved solids-not a recommended)

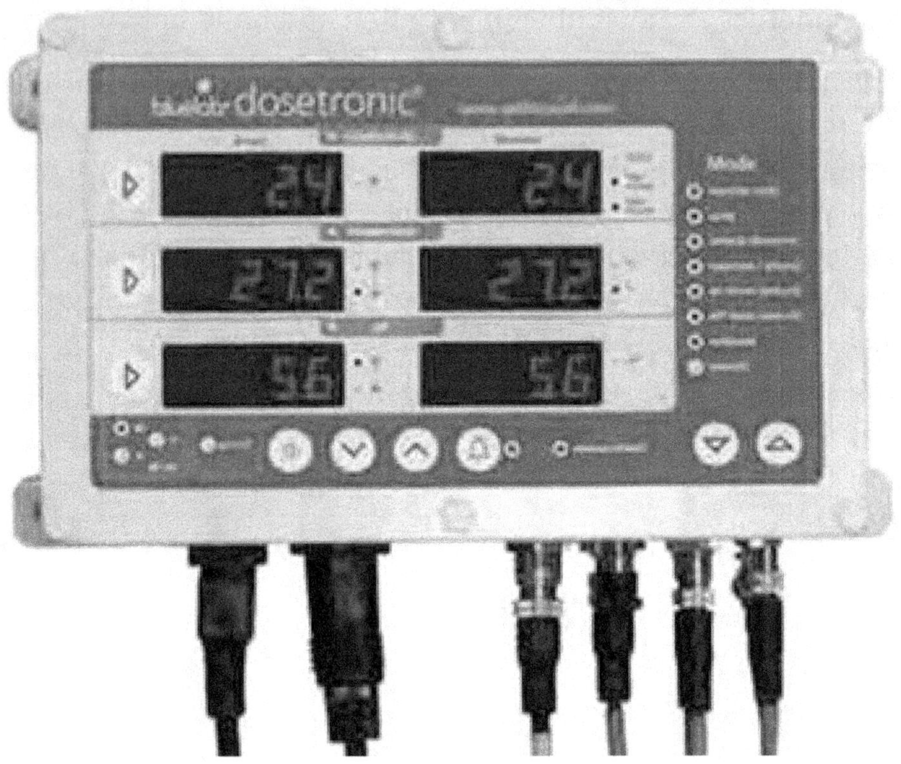

With the help of a CF meter, the hydroponic grower can quickly assess the strength of the mixture of nutrients and add more nutrients to the tank as needed. This may seem like a lot of work but note the plants that thrive in the soil also use nutrients. The difference is that you only detect nutrient deficiencies in plants grown in the soil when the symptoms of the deficiency appear and then it is almost too late. As a result, you must regularly apply fertilizers in quantities which are quite wasteful. In a hydroponic system only the nutrients actually used by the plants must be replaced. The plants may use huge amounts of nutrients but will yield phenomenal growth in doing so. Through adding automatic control systems, the performance of your hydroponic system may be taken a step further.

With an automatic CF controller you can pre-set the level of CF you want to maintain your system at. If plants use enough nutrients to enable the CF amount of the nutrient mixture to fall below the set level, the controller triggers a pump or solenoid valve automatically, causing further concentrate of nutrients to flow into the holding tank until the nutrient solution concentration falls above the set level and the dosing cycle is automatically shut down. Most CF controllers have alarms of high and low value, too. They will sound, warning you if, for example, your tank top up is empty, or if a valve or pump is defective. A professional grower with a large network would take the automatic controller seriously. Once installed, the only tasks left to the grower are pruning, harvesting and replacing the plants as well as refilling the topping up tanks occasionally. Even, CF controllers are good for home gardeners.

That means you can leave on holiday while your nutrient solution is automatically adjusted by the controller as needed. The control units now generated in New Zealand are responsible for controlling both CF and the other important indicator of your nutrient solution, pH. The control units are based on the CF and pH meters with additional controls that allow you to predetermine the levels of each required and to which the controller will adjust the nutrient solution to.

If you are willing to manually change the nutrient solution, a pH meter will be as useful as a CF meter to allow you to determine the state of the nutrient solution.

Only one pH meter, minimum hydroponic systems could be powered. For swimming pools you could use a color indicator tape or the type solution provided in kit form. The system works as long as the measure of color is in good condition. The only way to check that the indicator shows the true value is to try it out in a solution that you already know the pH value to see if the correct result is obtained. This is called a' buffer solution.' It's not usually worth trying to do without a proper pH meter, the outlay for a meter is minimal and the results are more accurate, especially if you have any color blindness.

The pH meter is basically a highly sensitive volt meter which measures the electricity pressure. Pure water has no voltage at all but there is a minute amount of electricity produced in both acidic and alkaline solutions. It is too small to be measured using a normal volt meter. The pH meter has a unique amplifier that increases the output of the pH probe that is placed in the measured solution. When amplified, the voltage signal generated in the probe is then modified by individual circuits to accommodate temperature variations as pH readings are influenced by temperature in the same way as the CF readings, but to a much smaller degree. The meter then provides a digital readout that shows you the pH value of the solution you tested.

The pH meter works by taking a minimal signal, multiplying it, adjusting it and then converting it to a pH level, so care must be taken to ensure accuracy of the readings when using the meter. The sample should be washed in purified or deionized water with a neutral pH value of 7.  The sample can then be tested by putting it in a buffer. The probe is first placed in a buffer solution that you know has a pH value of 7 The meter may not read 7 so that the buffer adjustment system has to be adjusted until the meter shows a pH reading of 7. The next step is to place the probe in a buffer solution with a pH value of 4 (or 10 it just needs to be offset from the neutral value of 7) so that the second adjustment is made. When dipped into your nutrient solution, the meter is now ready to give precise read.

The new meters have microprocessors in their circuits which make automatic calibration much simpler, so be sure to read the instructions provided with the meter to get the best performance from it. Ensure always to wash the probe in freshwater after reading on your pH meter.

Also you will need to keep the probe moist when it is not in use as the probe should never dry out. This procedure may seem complicated, but after you have your hydroponic garden established, you will find it only takes a few minutes of your time. Testing and adjusting your nutrient mixture regularly will give you good crops and take you far less time than weeding a conventional garden. Also remember that unlike a garden in the soil, a hydroponic garden can have its pH and CF levels tested and adjusted using automatic dosing equipment, some of the leading designs produced by New Zealand.

# CHAPTER FIVE
## Setting up a system

The basic steps involved when setting up a small growing area with an air pump have already been described. This system can be expanded although there are some points to be aware of as the size of your system increases. In an aggregate filled garden for example, you should check the drain and feeder pipes now and then to make sure that the plants' root systems have not blocked them up.

The larger system that you will be ready to set up now will also bring up a number of points that will be relevant to most large hydroponic systems. This can still be a simple system designed to supply several people and to run on a manual test system, however the step by step installation plan also includes the information needed to automate the system.

### Step One: Checking the Water Supply

The first and one of the most important steps to setting up any hydroponic system is to check the quality of your water supply. Water is the basis of the nutrient mixture, the central part of your whole hydroponic system. If your water is supplied by a local authority from a water treatment station then there will probably be no problems. You can check with your city engineers department who can usually supply you with a water analysis. If your water comes from a well or bore you should have a sample analyzed to make sure that the water is not overloaded with any element.

The maximum values of each element that plants can tolerate in parts per million are:

Sodium_________180 ppm

(if only growing lettuce this value should only
be 20ppm)

Calcium__________100 ppm

Chloride__________70 ppm

Boron____________0.2 ppm

Sulphate__________80 ppm

Magnesium________45 ppm

Carbonates_______60 ppm

The elements such as sodium, iron and zinc, for example, become toxic to plants if they are present in too high a concentration. Generally your water will be acceptable if the following values are not exceeded.

A water supply overloaded with one of the elements may be quite acceptable for human consumption yet prove to be unusable in a hydroponic system. If your water is one of the few cases where there is an impurity that cannot be filtered out, then you may have to consider an alternative water supply. Rainwater is often a good alternative.

**NOTE:** If levels are outside the values shown, then expert opinion should be sought to confirm both the formulae required and crops which would grow acceptably under such conditions.

If you wanted to grow plants hydroponically at a CF value of 25 for example and you were using water with an excess of sodium in it, you may find that the CF value of your nutrient solution is much higher than the 25 CF units you required.

This is because the water may have had a CF value of about 22 before you even added any nutrient mixture to it. The excess of sodium in your water supply would be responsible for this figure. This is just an example of one of the things that can happen if you fail to check your water supply before you start. Most hydroponic growers never experience this problem but it still pays to check.

Any containers that may not be inert should be painted with two coats of bituminous paint to make sure that they do not release any harmful substances into the nutrient solution.

Step Two: Planning the Layout of the Growing Area
The next step in setting up a hydroponic garden is to plan the layout of your gullies or growing areas. Keep the growing surface well above ground level. This will help you keep the produce clean and provides for good air circulation which is especially important if you are growing in a greenhouse. Always leave plenty of room between the growing areas so that you can get in to harvest your crops and put new plants in with ease. You can increase or decrease the size of the growing areas and alter their arrangement to suit your own situation so long as you adhere to some basic principles. The first is that the minimum fall for NFT gullies must be at least one in forty. Remember that this equals 1 cm of elevation at one end of the gully for every 40 cm of length. The flow to each gully should be around one litre per minute although experience will show you by how much you can reduce this figure. Pumping nutrient solution through your system at a faster rate than necessary would be a waste of electricity and could lead to undesirable ponding and root death..

The size and length of the NFT gullies will depend totally on the type of crop being grown. Lettuce for example, is not a big feeder, so gullies measuring 100 mm across, 50 mm high and anything up to 18 metres long can be used successfully.

Tomatoes, on the other hand, are very heavy feeders and also have a vigourous root structure which demands a good supply of oxygen and nutrients, so the length of the gully needs to be reduced. The use of excessively long gullies would result in the plants at the end of the gullies suffering poor root health. A good length of gully for tomatoes is 10 metres, although this can be extended up to 15 metres providing the gully is of sufficient size, is installed correctly to avoid any ponding of nutrient, has a minimum 1:40 slope and is provided with control of the flow rate to limit the volume of nutrient entering the gully.

Some growers use extra feeder pipes placed at intervals along extremely long gullies. This is not a recommended way to go about using longer gullies. You should always introduce all of your nutrient mixture at the head of the gully as the stale nutrient solution is expelled from the gully by the inflow of the replenished incoming nutrient solution. This may not happen as effectively when the inflow of nutrient solution is divided among a number of entry points. It would be better to use a larger number of gullies in short lengths with adequate flows. Remember how important oxygen is to the plants, the stale nutrient must be cycled back through to the holding tank effectively so that waste gases can be expelled and that the plants will receive fresh oxygen and nutrients.

A recent practice with NFT gullies has been to use a capillary mat to line the gully. This material acts like blotting paper, ensuring that the nutrient solution spreads over the whole floor of the gully. The permanent capillary mat is excellent in commercial situations where all of the plants and their root material are able to be removed at one time along with the mat. However with a hydroponic garden in the home, it can prove to be a nuisance when you only want to remove one plant, as the plant's roots will have grown right through the capillary mat. In most cases the mat is unnecessary except when the plants are extremely small. At this stage there is a chance that the plant's root system will not be in the path of the nutrient flow.

This problem is easily solved by placing either small pieces of paper towel underneath the roots of very small plants or a piece of the disposable capillary mat which dissolves after approximately ten days after first being wetted. These will act like blotting paper until the roots develop and the material gradually breaks up. The pieces of material are caught by a strainer which also removes any small particles of vegetation before they are flushed into the holding tank. This helps to keep the system clean.

Setting up aggregate filled containers is quite simple. The arrangement described in the section on growing containers using drums can be expanded until you reach the growing area you require or you can use large trays similar to those illustrated for the dual system in this chapter. The size of the aggregate filled containers can vary depending on the size of the holding tank you have room for. How you determine the size you need is fully explained in the section on holding tanks. Something you should remember to do when filling containers with aggregate is to use coarser material on the bottom which becomes finer as you fill the container up. Finish off with a layer of slightly coarser material on the surface. A layer lcm deep of 4mm or 5mm chip works well, allowing the surface layer to remain dry and free from algae growth.

## Step Three: The Holding Tank

The size of the holding tanks will depend on the size of the growing area to be supplied and on the type of system. Manual test and dose systems have different requirements from automatic dosing systems.

## Manual Systems

There is virtually no maximum size limit for holding tanks in manual test and dose systems, only a minimum size. The minimum size of the holding tank can be accurately established once you have your gullies, growing containers, feed and drain pipes and your pump set up and ready to operate. Select a container which you think will hold enough water to fill the system with an allowance for some extra water. You can then fill the container with water and start pumping it around the system while continuing to fill the container.

When all the gullies and growing containers have water flowing through them and back into the temporary holding tank you can stop filling it with water but keep the pump running so that water is still circulating through the system.

Now you can start slowly draining water out of the container until you reach the minimum amount needed to adequately service the pump. When you have reached this level stop draining and turn off the pump. Allow the water in the gullies and growing containers to drain back into your temporary holding tank. This will probably take from five minutes to half an hour after which time you will have the minimum quantity of water required to run the system in your tank.

Having discovered the minimum amount of liquid required to run your system you can obtain a holding tank of the appropriate size. You will be surprised how much water is in the system. If you fail to allow for the amount of water in the system when you decide on a size for the holding tank it will flood as soon as there is a power cut or if the pump fails.

The tank may still have to be able to hold considerably more liquid than the minimum amount you discovered in your trial run. Because when the system is operating complete with plants, the amount of nutrient solution in the system will have to be able to supply the nutritional requirements of all the plants for the time that passes in between tests and dosing.

The minimum amount of nutrient solution needed to keep liquid flowing through the system and to keep the pump operating could provide enough nutrients for the plants if you test and dose more regularly, say twice a day. In other words if you test and dose the mixture before breakfast and after your evening meal the minimum amount of nutrient mixture used will only have to keep the plants adequately nutritionally supplied for periods of about 10 hours.

If you decide that you only want to test and dose the mixture once a day it is going to have to last twice as long so a larger holding tank could/will be required. By using a larger tank than technically needed you will ensure that the plants will be kept adequately supplied especially during times of heavy feeding. Obviously considerations such as the effective use of the space you have available as well as finance will place some limit on the size of your holding tank although theoretically for manual systems this is a case of the bigger the better.

## Automatic Systems

The most efficient of all hydroponic systems is the automatically checked and dosed system. The simpler systems all work well but to retain their simplicity they sacrifice some aspect of performance. Without any test equipment at all you can grow hydroponically. Instead a volume of nutrient solution that is larger than actually required is completely replaced every two to three weeks.

Besides being wasteful, you must accept that, when you use this system, you will have no idea if there is enough food available to the plants throughout the entire time period. The disposal and substitution period can be extended widely through the use of automated test equipment, but there will still be periods when the nutrient does not provide the best possible growth because its mechanism may have gone well out of control over time.

You'll have noticed how irritable humans become when they miss a regular meal. Which makes you think it's any different plants. Therefore the maximum device dosage on demand 24 hours a day, This will ensure, for example, that plants such as tomatoes, which can be found absorbing nutrients at 1 am in the morning, always have the nutrients they require.

The size of the nutrient solution carrying tank must be thoroughly matched to the lowest possible liquid demands of the hydroponic system to obtain the highest possible efficiency from an automatic testing and dosing controller. As with manually tested and adjusted systems, there is no room for going to excessively large holding tanks. This is because the automated system will have greater power over a smaller amount of solution of nutrients. For example, if you were running a system automatically set to be kept at a level of 25

C F units, you might find the nutrient solution's temperature rises by up to 10 ° C during the day.

For this rise, the heat from the sun would be largely responsible, and every degree celsius that the temperature rises changes the nutrient mixture's CF value by two percent. Remember, the apparent CF value is affected by temperature. Automatic CF controllers have a temperature sensing circuit that compensates for any changes in temperature and effectively keeps the CF at the desired value, however there are problems with large capacity holding tanks that are dosed up to the desired CF value. If the temperature varies so much the system can not keep pace with the changes. Where necessary, the controller may increase the dosage but can not reduce it.

Automatic systems rely on the plants to lower the nutrient solution's CF value by using up the nutrients. The plants would soon use enough nutrients in a system with a small holding tank to lower the CF value, but this could take a long time in a large capacity tank. In some cases the temperature may again have changed before this was achieved. The variations in temperatures between night and day can often be extreme enough to cause this problem. The alternative is for the storage tank to be designed on the same level as the manual method. This lowest possible size should not be exceeded to ensure that the CF and pH values for nutrient solutions are kept as accurate as possible.

The system will only use enough water to keep the growing areas supplied and the pump submerged in the holding tank so you will have to make sure this level does not drop further. You can do this by adjusting the water make up valve so that as soon as the level drops below the required level new water flows in. Remember that the CF value could also rise to a critical level if you allow the water can be used up without replacing it in time. If there is too strong a reverse osmosis in the nutrient solution, the plants will lose their moisture, wilt and die.

## Step Four: Installing an Automatic Controller

The first and, one of the most important points to remember about installing an automatic controller is to locate it away from water, dirt or any other elements that are liable to affect the operation of the unit. Humid conditions should be avoided so a well ventilated structure should be built to house the controller away from the holding tanks and growing area. You could still house it in the same room as the holding tanks, if the conditions were favourable with the controller mounted on a wall away from any splashes or drips. You can start installing the controller by fitting a pipe into the main nutrient supply pipe just as it leaves the holding tank. A tap should be fitted at this point so that the control system can be shut off and worked on without having to close the whole system down. The pipe runs from the main nutrient pipe to a small sample container next to the automatic controller, wherever it has been located.

A 16mm PVC pipe will be large enough to take a sample of some of the nutrient solution up to this container. A CF inline cell can be fitted into this pipe and connected to the automatic controller. To ensure that the CF cell produces accurate readings install the cell inclined on a 45° angle with a non return valve on the supply side, use secure fittings on either side to prevent air leaks. Any pockets of air that form in the cell will produce inaccurate readings. The automatic controller will also have a connection for a temperature compensating probe for the CF reading. This probe can be placed either in the main holding tank or the sample container. Some controllers do away with inline cells and simply use a 'dip' type probe complete with its own temperature thermistor placed into the sample container.

The next item to install is the pH probe which is installed in the sample container. This container should have an inlet fitting at the bottom and an outlet drain back to the holding tank at the top. The pH dosing line will also feed into the sample container. You will remember from the chapter on equipment, it was stressed that pH probes should never be allowed to dry out once they have been put into operation.

The glass measuring bulb has to be kept wet and clean. Both of these requirements can be easily satisfied by connecting the pH dosing line to the sample container so that it pours acid onto the pH probe. Nitric and phosphoric acid are usually used to alter the pH of the nutrient solution. Acid is also the best substance for cleaning the pH probe. This arrangement allows a fine control of the overall nutrient pH value because as soon as acid is pumped into the sample container it hits the pH probe connected to the automatic controller. The probe will send a signal to the controller which immediately shuts off the supply of acid avoiding overdosing.

The second requirement is achieved by setting the input pipe to the sample container above the height of the bulb end of the pH probe so that even if the sample container was to drain out, a residual amount would still be enough to keep the probe wet

The nutrients flow from the holding tank through feed pipes into the growing containers and drain back in an automatically controlled system in the same way as in a manual. A line is conducted from the main feed pipe and a sample of the nutrient solution is taken to check. This line contains a shutdown tap to allow you to turn off the automatic system if necessary. The feed line is connected to an inline CF measuring cell that is connected at an angle of 45 ° to prevent air bubbles that give false readings. The CF cell tells the automatic controller when the nutrient solution is too weak and the controller activates the operating solenoid valves (or pumps), allowing extra nutrients to flow into the main holding tank from the top up tanks. The pH of the nutrient mixture is measured using a pH probe located in the sample container of the nutrient solution located behind the CF cell. When the pH is too high the controller activates an air pump which pressures the holding acid tank used to adjust the nutrient's pH level. Acid flows up the pipe into the sample container mixing with the nutrient solution that continually flows back down an overflow pipe to the main holding tank. The system also features a water make-up valve that allows additional water to flow into the holding tank as the volume drops too low.

A pipe that will be able to resist the acid (PVC-Polythene) should connect the holding tank for the acid to the sample containers. To force the acid up into the sample container, a small aquarium air pump may be used. This pump is connected to the automatic controller and is activated by the controller if the pH probe senses a nutrient solution pH rise.

The pump works by pressing the liquid in the bottle pushing water up the pipe into the tube, which changes the nutrient solution's pH. The automated controller triggers a pump or solenoid valve equally for feeding nutrients into the central holding tank. The controller activates the pump when it receives a signal from the CF cell which indicates that the nutrient solution's strength has fallen. When the CF cell senses an increase in nutrient solution intensity to the amount preset on the device, the pump is turned off.

The principles and operation of an automatically controlled system are quite simple making the arrangement something that both the home grower and the commercial grower can accomplish. When you start to grow with a manually checked and dosed device you will become fully familiar with the equipment for CF and pH checks. This will make it easier to install automatic control equipment when you decide to have an understanding of how the test equipment operates. In an automatic system, the pH check probe will have to be buffered once a week and the CF probe washed every three to four months with an acceptable cleaner, Jiff, Soft scrub or patented cleaning substance.

Besides these regular checks all the grower will have to do once an automatic system is in place, note to empty the nutrient topping up tanks and the tank full of acid to change the nutrient solution's pH. Remember that if everything else fails please read the installation and operating instructions issued by the manufacturer of the equipment.